Animal Opposites

by David Bauer

STECK-VAUGHN

A Harcourt Company

www.steck-vaughn.com

How are these animals opposites?

The whale is **BIG.**

2

The fish is *small*.

How are these animals opposites?

The snake is long.

The frog is short.

How are these animals opposites?

The sheep has *curly* hair.

The goat has straight hair.

One dog has **light** fur.
The other dog has **dark** fur.